The Healing Power of Seashells
Daya Sarai Chocron

the Healing Power *of* Seashells

Daya Sarai Chocron

EARTHDANCER

A FINDHORN PRESS IMPRINT

Publisher's note

The information in this volume has been compiled according to the best of our knowledge and belief. Bearing in mind that different people react in different ways, neither the publisher nor the author can give a guarantee for the effectiveness or safety of use in individual cases. In the case of serious health problems please consult your doctor or naturopath.

1 2 3 4 5 6 7 17 16 15 14 13 12 10 09 08 07 06 05

Daya Sarai Chocron
The Healing Power of Seashells

With photos by Gaby Gad, Joseph Weeler, Franz Späth (p 27)
and Ines Blersch (Appendix)

This English edition © 2005 Earthdancer Books
Original English text © 2005 Daya Sarai Chocron

Published by Earthdancer Books, an imprint of:
Findhorn Press · 305a The Park · Findhorn · Forres IV36 3TE · Great Britain

Editing of the text by Roselle Angwin

Book jacket, original graphics, artwork and typesetting by Dragon Design, GB
Typeset in ITC Cleargothic
Cover photography: Comstock, Fotosearch.com
Printed and bound by Legoprint S.p.A., Italy.

ISBN 1-84409-068-X

*In deep gratitude to Mother Sea
and to my three jewels:
Matthew, Rachel and Anna*

Contents

Introduction

Nearly twenty years ago I arrived in Capoliveri, a charming village on a hill on the island of Elba in Italy, to spend the winter. I had just begun to teach in Europe that autumn, and was graciously offered a house by a friend. This house overlooks the Tyrrhenian Sea, and receives the daily sacrament of the magnificent sunset, the 'Tramonto' (Italian word for Sunset).

It is now December 2001 and I am back here, in the same house, admiring the glorious colours of the sun as it sets in the distant hills of Corsica. What a rich and rewarding journey it has been since that winter of 1983 – a journey of awakening, light, love, life, tolerance, creativity, and freedom.

Here, I started putting my notes together for my first book *Healing with Crystals and Stones,* finishing it later that year in Provence in the South of France, in the picturesque village of La Roche St. Secret – The Rock of the Holy Secret. Later, during a conference in Austria, a woman who was to become a great sister again offered me her house, surrounded by lavender fields, to complete the book.

Many moons ago, while still living in the Southwest of Arizona, New Mexico, the crystals and stones asked me to go out and teach and be an 'ambassador' for them. I travelled and taught throughout Europe in Germany, Switzerland, Austria, France and Italy, sharing the sacredness of this work.

There has been a rediscovery of and openness towards the mineral kingdom, Mother Earth and alternative therapies. More and more people have become aware of the inter-relatedness of life in our world. This indeed is the Prasad,* the sweet reward, the gift: to have participated and lived as an instrument of awareness and guardianship for our Mother Earth.

During those years my inner seeking took me to distant lands and to numerous teachers, and it was in Hawaii, in the island of Kauai, that I was blessed with the sacred teachings of healing with seashells.

Always I return to the places of Nature for nurturing my heart, my body, my Self. I walk; this grounds me, relaxes me, and opens me. As I walk I stand on Mother Earth, as a sentient human, a bridge, my heart in the sky, my eyes and heart open to unlimited beauty. I walk to the sea and fill myself up with the blue. I breathe in the blue of the sky and the blue of the sea – the blue of empty space. I become calm and peaceful; there I recover my wings and my spirit soars.

I honour our two mothers – Mother Earth and Mother Sea – both so nourishing, healing, beautiful and powerful.

Blessings

Daya Sarai Chocron
('Shining Moon')
Capoliveri, Island of Elba,
Italy Dec. 2001 – 2002

*Prasad is a sweet treat given, in India, to the disciple by the teacher after a ritual or ceremony, as a reward.

> *'We live on Earth to celebrate our life in unison with the universe.'*
> Native American Shaman

As we extend our awareness, we come to realise that the whole planet is a being. The Cosmos is a being; it has beingness. Matter is solidified energy. Therefore mountains and rivers and trees and oceans are energy, just like you and me.

The devastating ecological imbalance and the loss of health that we are undergoing is due to our illusion that the human race is superior to the other non-human beings, with whom we live and inhabit and share the planet.

Life was not created by mankind. It is a beginningless and endless phenomenon. The Cosmos, which is composed of innumerable universes, is not a creation of human thought or hand. Its interrelatedness is the essence of existence. We may plant a seed and help the seed to sprout, to grow into a sapling, into a tree by watering it and caring for it, but the creative energy hidden in that tiny seed or pit is not our creation.

Therefore the mountains, the rivers, the trees, the oceans are our fellow companions, our relatives with whom we share the Cosmos. We share the skies with them, the oceans with them, the earth with them.

There is sacredness because there is unconditionedness – purity and divine vibrating intelligence in every being. This all-permeating

Intelligence, the energy of Intelligence, has resulted in harmony and order. When we recognise that the Supreme Intelligence as an Energy permeates us all – you, me, every living being – we are able to be at peace. We are back in our wholeness – the source of being. For billions of years this planet's life has been manifesting itself into innumerable forms, each form having its unique beauty and relevance to the wholeness of life.

Life is a magnificent wholeness. Even a drop of water contains the mystery of the wholeness of life. The awareness of interrelatedness awakens the tenderness of love and compassion. The Sacred is the divinity of all life.

> '*God said,*
> *let the waters bring forth swarms of living creatures.'*
> Genesis 1:20

For as long as I can remember the sea has fascinated me. It is a place of mystery – a timeless elemental world of water and sky and great winds. Its shimmering beauty, its diamond-like sparkle of sun on water, the scent at the sea's edge, the feeling of vast movements of water, the sound of waves have all, since my childhood, created a need in me to return to the sea time and time again for solace, for contemplation, for nurturing and nourishment, and for inspiration.

I grew up by the sea, feeling very early on a great love for natural beauty. I sensed the ocean as an overall dominating force. It is a place that is always changing and seems changeless; linking us from the beginning of time to the present now. Spending hours in the dunes, on a beach, on the rocks, feeling the mysterious and brooding spirit of the deep and hidden waters. The sea's face always mobile, sensitive; the continually changing light and colours – are for me, the mystery of life itself revealed.

Water is a pure, potential and unformed matrix from which all life takes its being. For hundreds of millions of years, all life was sea life, giving birth to a prodigious, abundant variety of creatures, some of which crept out of the sea onto solid earth. We carry the sea's salt in our blood, as well as a memory of our marine heritage.

In the wide immensity of the sea we come to understand its awesome power, its sublime sacredness. Everywhere the wind and the sea shape the coast, sculpting it into forms that are often magical, beautiful, and sometimes strange; even creating caves in the sea cliffs. In every grain of sand is the story of the earth.

The true spirit of the sea can be experienced on a lonely shore at dawn or at sunset, or in a storm or midnight darkness; there we see that the sea has nothing to do with humanity. Its spirit is beyond our comprehension of time and space.

'Patience, patience, patience is what the sea teaches.
Patience and faith. One should lie empty, open, choiceless
as a beach, waiting for a gift of the sea.'
Anne Morrow Lindbergh

The Legend of the Sands

A fairytale by Halka, a Sufi Master from Arabia

In a Kingdom far from other mountains a white transparent river was born. During her existence she made a long journey, travelling through various countries of vast and fertile valleys. Finally, she arrived at the sands of an immense desert. She had met many obstacles and she had always known how to overcome them. From the hardest rocks she had made soft and round pebbles, which sang along her path.

She tried to go through this last obstacle in her usual manner. Great was her surprise when she realised that all the art and science she possessed were of no help. Her waters disappeared in the sands as quickly as she threw them in. She tried again and again, and despair began to overtake her. Yet she continued to throw her waters into the sands, within the immense silence of the desert.

And then, from the depths of the sands, arose the murmur of a voice which whispered: 'The wind crosses the desert, and in the same way the river can also.'

The river responded that this is what she was trying to do, but that she was exhausted: 'I have only been able to lose myself each time a little more, and am still only at the edge of this desert.' She added: 'The wind can fly, that is why he can cross the desert.'

'If you continue to throw yourself with violence, as you have been,' replied the sands, 'you will not be able to cross.

You must disappear, or you will become a swamp. Allow the wind to carry you to your destiny.'

'But how can I do this?' asked the river.

'Accept the idea of being absorbed by the wind,' answered the murmur.

This idea did not please the river. She had never yet been absorbed. In addition she was afraid to lose her individuality: 'And once I have disappeared, how will I regain my identity? When will I be a river again?'

'The wind, the wind,' whispered the sands, 'he will accomplish his function. He lifts the waters, carries them above the desert, and then releases them as rain, which again forms a river.'

'But,' exclaimed the river, 'how do I know that what you say is true?'

'It is so,' said the voice again, from the bottom of the sands, 'and if you don't believe it you will become a swamp. This will take years. And you know a swamp of stagnant water is quite different from a flowing river.'

'But can't I remain just as I am now?' implored the river.

'No, it is impossible,' whispered the sands. 'You cannot keep your actual form. But your essence will be carried and will become a river again.'

'But,' complained the river again, 'I don't even know what my essence is.'

This time there was no answering voice from the desert.

Eventually the words of the sands began to resonate in the

memory of the river. Some strange remembrance echoed, as if some part, a piece of herself, had already been carried by the wind. It seemed to remind her that all this had to happen, that she needed to live out her destiny even if she had no desire to do so.

As the river stopped resisting, her waters were lifted up as steam into the receiving arms of the wind, who softly inhaled her essence.

He carried her swiftly far away to a very high peak in the distant kingdom of the mountains.

There the river awoke to her beingness, where resonated still the echo of the voice that came from the sands: 'We, the sands, know the path that lies ahead at the end of the rivers, leading to the faraway kingdom of the mountains.'

This is why it is said: the river of life is a path and its destiny is written in the sands.

The Water Element

> *'There is nothing constant in the universe,*
> *All is ebb and flow, and every shape that's born,*
> *bears in its womb the seeds of change.'*
> Ovid (Metamorphoses)

The Sea – the ebb and the flow
The waves crashing on the shore
Riding the waves or going under
The rivers, the ponds, the lakes, the glaciers, the snow
The Rain
The Waterfalls
The Source – the Well
Drinking pure water, washing, purifying, cleansing
The tears – the depth of feelings and emotions
Transparency – Fluidity

I invite you to close your eyes and visualise the water element within you. Are you floating on a calm surface? Or are you diving into deep waters? Are you refreshing yourself under a waterfall? Are you walking in the rain? Or are you dancing underwater? Are you a mermaid? Is your water cold or pleasant to your body? The invigorating North Seas or balmy South Seas? Are you crying from joy, beauty, or sorrow? Do you feel thirsty? Are you flowing? Or contracting?

We are born of water in our mother's womb, and in many cultures water is considered our first mother. We are made up of 70% of liquid – our body needs it to survive, in order not to dehydrate. We resonate to water. Our breath carries the flux of change, just like the ebb and the flow. Every inhalation that we take is a new one and with the exhalation we throw out what we had inhaled a moment ago.

In all rituals and ceremonies, in all cultures, water is seen as a purifying force. In India the day begins with the ritual of the bath, ablutions, prayers. In Islamic tradition people wash their feet and their hands before entering a mosque to pray to Allah. In Christianity there is the ritual of Baptism, where the whole being is immersed in water to be 'reborn'.

A long time ago I dreamed that I had to jump into the turbulent waters of a wild sea. I went under, was rolled about, and finally emerged naked and clean.

I understood it to symbolise the passions, the emotions, the fears – thus the myth of Venus, who is rolled about in the ocean and emerges naked – open, loving – as the Goddess.

The purification of perception, the purging of conditioning, and the washing out of toxins all lead to communion with what is, and allow spontaneity and liberation.

To be able to float is a truly liberating experience; to let go of the weight of the body, the heavy baggage we all carry.

Water, as in the Tao, teaches us to flow, to go around obstacles instead of hitting them head-on. We so often bang ourselves against walls, instead of being fluid. Water will seep through and under the earth and come out in another place.

The source, the well, are metaphors of life. The I Ching describes water as the deep, inexhaustible, divinely centred source of nourishment and meaning for humanity. The original Chinese text depicts hexagram 48 as The Well. It states: 'The town may be changed, but the well cannot be changed. It cannot be increased or decreased.'

People may explore various philosophies, scholarly pursuits, spiritual disciplines, altering their awareness in myriad ways; yet still they must always return to the source of their true nature for fulfilment.

The Source contains and is born of the collective truth of humanity. It receives from the individual's experience and gives to the individual nature.

To put a bowl of water on an altar is to invite abundance in our life. Because of water all things grow.

Water can take several forms and yet return to its true nature. The streamlets dash out of the mountain rocks and grow into rivers; the rivers pour their water into the oceans and the heat of the sun converts the salty water into desalinated vapours and clouds, and the clouds pour their sweet nectar, the water, back to our Earth. This cycle demonstrates that life is an inexhaustible font of creative energy.

In particularly dry climates, fountains and pools of water in the garden were regarded as life giving, not only for the body, but also for the soul. They were places where people would go and sit and contemplate the water.

I remember sitting by an exquisite pool in contemplation in the magnificent Moorish palace, the Alhambra in Granada, Spain, when a guardian came and asked me humbly if I was meditating. I smiled and said I was admiring. He then showed me the way the light would reflect in the water at a certain angle and said that its purpose was to reflect the Light of God!

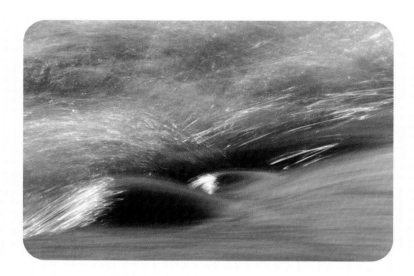

Transparency – reflection of the light – that we may be vessels of light.

In the Southwest of Arizona, New Mexico, during drought season, festivals are held to ask for the blessing of water so that crops will grow, so that people will live. The prayers for water are prayers for life.

Masters in Ancient Greece would take their disciples to a body of water and there would test their inner tranquillity. Inner and outer were to be brought into harmony.

Water is also traditionally used for scrying in many cultures. Priestesses, clairvoyants and seers would read omens in the waters – either in a vessel, well or pool or in the sea – during a full moon or at other special times of the year.

In the Tarot deck, card number XIV in the Major Arcana is Temperance. She holds two vessels in which a white stream of liquid flows from one vase to the other. It symbolises the knowledge of continuity, exchange, circulation of fluids, and cosmic movement. The vase represents the maternal breast in which there is universal rebirth – the promise of unending life.

The most revered of the four great gods of old Hawaii, Lono, was the supreme god of peace and fertility. He was a god of the sea, clouds, winds, agriculture, and fertility. Today, Lono is looked to as the god of peace and prosperity, offering the promise of a wealth of life's blessings.

May your cup run over!

'One cannot step twice in the same river,
for fresh waters are forever
flowing around us.'
Heraklitus

Shell Dance

'The cure for anything is saltwater:
sweat, tears, or the sea.'
Isak Dinesen

When I arrived in the spectacular island of Kauai early in 1997, I opened my centre, 'Shamballah*', and hosted a series of weekly classes in seashell healing. Little did I know at the outset what a blessing that would be in my life, and how these teachings would become a central force during my years there, and continuing still today.

It is with infinite gratitude to my friend and teacher Lin C. Hansen, her teacher, and the 'Grandmothers' that I acknowledge these ancient teachings and wish to pass on their heritage.

The house was perfectly situated on the beach, where the sound of the waves, the voice of the sea, the music of swelling power that swirls and explodes all became intimate companions. The daily contemplation of the sea, its reflection of the sky, its magic at full moon, its quality of transparency – all this had a presence so vast that no human words can convey this adequately.

* Shamballah is said to be a hidden paradisaical centre of wisdom and peace in the highlands of Asia. 'Shamballah' was the name given to me by my guides for my centres. For me it means 'Temple of Peace'

Shell energy was introduced to Lin by her spirit-guide teacher whom she called Tutu Keolani. (Her full name – Keolani Kekaiiwe Makanea – means 'The precious Life of the Sea-Bones'.)

During my own work and meditations with seashells the Grandmothers bestowed on me 'Kanele'a Inui Lei' – 'The joyful garland of sharing Sacred Words'.

The wisdom of the healing energy of seashells comes to us from the ancient Island peoples. A few years ago the Grandmothers began to share this knowledge again. They said that seashells are tangible aspects of the feminine or goddess energy that can benefit both men and women, allowing the balancing of our male and female aspects. (Healing here means a return to Harmony.)

For so many years my work has been dedicated to crystals and stones from Mother Earth; and here I was blessed with being able to experience their sisters, the seashells from Mother Sea – a union of the gifts from the natural world.

Seashells – their History and Uses

Seashells are the hard outer covering of highly adapted snails that inhabit the world's oceans in a wide range of environments and at varying depths. These shells can be found washed ashore, emptied of the soft bodies that once lived in them, in rock pools, beneath mud and sand at low tide, and beneath the sea in shallow water. In scientific terms they are known as marine molluscs. They are of great interest in relation to environmental ecological issues, as well as in medical research and general education. They have always been an important food source, and are linked to a relatively new field of research called mariculture. The study and collecting of shells is known as conchology. As we increase our awareness of the need for environmental protection, there is also a growing need to discover

more about our natural world; this, I believe, helps enhance our connection to all life.

It has always been a thrill for me to walk along the shore and come upon seashells, still wet from the waves. My heart sings; nowhere else am I so happy, so fully 'with' the element and in the present moment.

These exquisite wonders of creation have been inextricably linked with the human story since the dawn of civilisation. We are intrigued and amazed at their diversity and complexity of colour, design, shape and form. There is still today an appreciation and enjoyment of collecting sea shells, in adults as well as children; and seashells have always inspired artists, poets and musicians, as well of course as being an influence in design and architecture.

Currency and Trade

In ancient cultures the cowrie shells were used for currency and trade in Asia, Central Africa, the Indian Ocean, and the Malaysian islands. Because they were easy to collect and handle, they were strung into lengths and use for bartering. Early traders made fortunes by carrying cowries from the Indian and Pacific Oceans to West Africa, where they were exchanged for ivory, palm oil, and semi-precious stones. These shells have been discovered in aboriginal sites in parts of the U.S, which suggests that they may have been imported, perhaps even before the time of Columbus.

The North American Indians used to grind down pieces of bivalves and also use them for trading. Certain clams were pierced and strung on sinew, the most prized shells having a purple interior.

American Indian traders journeyed from the coast to inland villages trading abalone, tusk shells, and others for jewellery and for their dye secretions; especially prized were shells that provided the colour purple.

Fashion and Jewellery

Shells have been used for adornment from the earliest times in Africa, India, the Middle East, Asia, the Americas, Australia, and Europe. Cowries, which were consecrated to the Goddess Venus, were worn by Roman women and were often given as bridal gifts.

Clothes were often embellished with shells. The fashion for shell jewellery and ornamental objects included haircombs, earrings, brooches and necklaces exquisitely fashioned out of mother-of-pearl and other nacreous oysters. In Oriental artefacts we find much furniture, such as chests, tables, room dividers, chairs and so on, made with inlays of mother-of-pearl. In Victorian times shell-backed mirrors and perfume bottles were highly popular. Cameos were carved into the thick walls of the shells through layers of rich orange, red, and off-white.

Art and Architecture

Of all shells, the scallop has perhaps been the most frequently used – ornamenting Roman coffins, decorating niches and porticoes, carved above church doorways. It is also the Pilgrim symbol, dedicated to St James; travellers on the ancient Camino of Santiago de Compostella wore it as they made the pilgrimage from all over Europe to the shrine of St James in Compostella, Spain. It was chosen by Sandro Botticelli (1445–1510) as a vehicle for the birth of Venus rising from the Sea – an allusion to goddess energy.

The chambered nautilus inspired the famous architect Fibonacci, known for the Golden Mean Spiral, because of the mathematical precision in its perfectly balanced chambers. Leonardo Da Vinci made drawings of these spiral shells, providing the inspiration for the famous spiral staircase at the Chateau de Blois, in France.

In the 16th and 17th centuries the Dutch became great collectors of exotic shells. This passion is reflected in Rembrandt's etchings 'The Shell' and in Vanders Ast's 'Still Life with Shells'.

Religion

The conch, sacred to the Hindu god Vishnu, was sometimes covered with gold and encrusted with precious jewels. In India and Sri Lanka (Ceylon) conch shells are blown to signal the 'Opening of the Heavens' at the beginning of a ceremony, especially at sunrise.

In the Hawaiian tradition, all ceremonies and healings commence with the blowing of the conch, a calling of the Spirit, a cleansing of space and aura; something I too had to learn and which I utilise in my healing rituals.

A Natural Healing Tool

As shells were used by early woman and man as receptacles, cooking utensils, tools, adornments, implements for ceremony and ritual, it was natural for people living close to the sea to look to shells to facilitate their own healing.

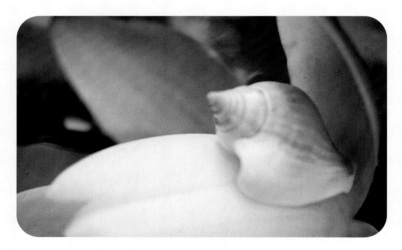

So seashells have been a natural part of the evolutionary process on this planet. They have evolved and changed for over two billion years.

Our physical bodies are composed of 70% water (for children it is closer to 90%). The oceans cover about 70–80% of the surface of the Earth; no surprise, then, that we are greatly influenced by the water element.

The sea calls us with her rhythm of waves and tides. She gives us the gift of shells or 'Sea Bones' of the creatures that grow them as part of their own creative protection.

Natural beauty has a necessary place in the spiritual development of every person. There is in us a deeply seated response to the natural universe, which is part of our humanity. There we are rewarded with the blessings of calmness, courage, patience, endurance, beauty, and luminosity.

We are part of the whole stream of life – built of the same elements as air, water, rock.

'Be at peace as you enter the deep waters of change.'

Shells are a wonderful source of energy for relieving tension and stress in the body. They contain the essence of the powerful yet subtle energies of the oceans which nurture our planet. Their resonance facilitates the opening to a greater awareness for our nature, and creates the feeling of harmony in our minds, hearts, and bodies.

Stress causes our bodies to tense, restricting both physical and emotional movement. Relaxation allows the natural energy flow to return. The longer we are under stress without relaxing, the more difficult it is for the body to remember its natural state.

Shell patterns, which suggest movement and flow, are a physical reminder for our bodies to return to their natural flow, similar to that of the ocean.

Shells offer themselves to us. They come into yet another cycle of life when we use them. They seem to come alive as we become their willing partners in creating harmony in our lives.

These wondrous beauties of the sea come to us from the deep as tools of transformation and sacredness. Their dance of energy is to release tension and facilitate change.

The 'Grandmothers' are the keepers of the legacy of the ancient continent of Lemuria. Their teachings speak of the ocean's shells as tools to help us journey deep underwater, into the unconscious forces that lie beneath the surface of everyday awareness: our own deep waters of emotions, feelings, dreams, in rhythm with the mysterious cycles of the Moon. As we do this so we can be released and freed.

The greatest gift that the seashell's Dance of Energy bestows upon us is the gift of rejuvenation – becoming whole and new again; clear, energised, inward, in contact with the Source, in awareness of Beingness.

> *'Life is ever moving, changing, laughing, playing, ever into the new.'*

Shell patterns can be divided into two main categories with regard to their energy.

Radiant Energy Shells

In this category we find many shells of the bivalve family including scallops, mussels, clams and cockle shells; in fact, all of the hinged shells. Limpets and corals are classified as radiant shells as well, even though they are not bivalves. Looking at their designs we can see the radiating lines that move from a central core outward.

These radiant shells are used for releasing blocks and increasing energy flow. They emanate a very soft, subtle type of energy, creating an effective pathway to the 'openness' and 'beingness' of the feminine aspect of our nature. This unfolding allows the opportunity to be receptive to internal transformation, which brings us into readiness for our next step in life. Life is ever moving, changing, laughing, playing, flowing into the new. These shells are wonderful to use when travelling to cities as they help us to remain balanced, relaxed, and flowing.

Spiral Energy Shells

These are the gastropods, or main shells. Single rather than double-shelled, they are twisted or coiled around a central core in a spiral design. Included in this category are the conch, cowries, cones, murex, tritons, whelks, augers, abalone, screwshells, and many more. We shall also include the chambered nautilus in the spiral work.

The pattern they contain is a spiral running from the centre point or apex around the core in a clockwise direction, and of course if the movement is begun at the opening or aperture and the spiral is followed, it will move in a counter-clockwise direction. The direction of the spiral is important because it will determine the effect. To create change we use the counter-clockwise movement. To increase the existing energy in a pattern, we focus on the effectiveness of the clockwise movement.

The spiral shell's energy is more intense than the energy of the radiant shell as its purpose is to use the 'point' – the centre of pain, almost in the way that a crystal quartz does.

We find the spiral in many formations in Nature, which suggests that spiral forms belong to a higher overall order. In the spiral we find a continuum whose opposite ends symbolise a coming from and returning to the source. Thus the windings of the spiral make it a symbol of eternity. Teilhard de Chardin has called this the Omega Point: 'The psychical convergence of the universe upon itself'. The path of consciousness is seen as a journey out and a return along the same path. (The spiral maze or labyrinth echoes this idea.) All mani-festations extend from, and yet are contained within, the point, to which it also returns. We could see this as a manifestation of the Goddess, who contains everything within herself. The spiral tendency within each one of us is the longing for and growth towards wholeness.

Every whole is a cycle, and has a beginning, a middle and an end. It starts from a point, expands, differentiates, contracts and disap-pears into the point once more. Such a pattern is that of our lifetime and that of our universe. Each person who is integrated, self-realised and truly individualised becomes universal. Thus the extreme point of differentiated individual consciousness leads back to our totality.

The *Tao Te Ching says:*
'Going on means going far.
Going far means returning.'

Each shell has its own unique form of communication through its individual design.

Radiant Shells

Scallops and Cockles

These are flowing, relaxing, wonderful to use on joints such as shoulders and knees to release blocks; they are useful for any congested area, as they will move energy. They come in lovely colours and make for beautiful 'spreads' or layouts.

These shells contain a blueprint, a memory pattern of natural harmony. In layouts they aid in clearing congested cellular patterns and help us to heal faster, to be clear about where we want to go, to experience from the depths of our soul the deep nurturing and the return. This 'homecoming' is a coming home from the depth of our soul, radiating out from the sacred centre.

In Kauai I was fortunate enough as to find a 'sunrise' shell, so named because of its lovely pinks graduating to golds. Later I had it set, together with a Herkimer diamond (quartz), and I wear it next to my heart, especially when I travel, to carry the beauty of the sea.

Corals and Sea Bones

N.B. As coral is now a species threatened with extinction, please read the chapter 'Information on Threatened Species'.

Red Coral

The red colour aids in any problems with blood or bleeding, especially with menstrual cramps and heavy flow. Red coral's 'organ pipes' resemble blood vessels. Coral is a gift from our mother ocean to remind us of our fundamental nature. It is actually composed of the skeletons of tiny animals, compressed into a reef which is plant-like, with hardened branches. It reminds us of our bones – hard and durable. In shamanic traditions the bones were considered to be the essence of man. Coral teaches us form, also flow and flexibility within form. It lives and breathes in the sea but its roots are anchored in the earth.

It is one of the sacred gems of the Tibetans, and the American Indians. It symbolises life-force energy. It was used as a protection against the evil eye.

Coral has an absorbing quality, and turns pale if the wearer is anaemic or deficient in 'blood' energy. In terms of healing, the darker reds are heating, revitalising and stimulating to the blood-stream and the entire body. The pink shades have a more direct influence on the heart by restoring harmony where there is a conflict of emotions.

It is good to wear in cases of nutritional deficiency, depression, or lethargy. Red coral is very much connected to women and birth. Used on the first chakra, or placed between the feet, it is also effective for grounding.

Mushroom Coral

From the centre point, all radiating lines in this truly lovely white coral speak of staying both centred and connected with energy. The centre principle manifests itself through us in the same way as it

does in a flower or a star and in this coral, so that we may discover our cosmic community.

The expanding energy of mushroom coral helps us to open to new levels and new understanding. By concentrating our energy we are able to heal ourselves, grow and expand.

Mushroom coral helps heal broken bones, and will also help relieve tension when placed in or on an area of discomfort.

It is superb for tired feet, and also good to use on top of the head.

It can also be used for clearing stones and jewellery simply by laying the latter on it.

Spiral Shells

Cowrie

The cowrie comes in all sizes from small to medium to large in an array of colours and patterns. Sometimes it is pure white with earthy colours inside, much like an egg. Its inner spiral conveys a womb, closely associated with cocooning and nurturing. It carries a soft female energy excellent for comforting and 'going within'.

Cowries are great to use for massages, on their soft shiny side, all over the body, especially the neck and the feet. They can also be used to 'scoop out' excess nervous energy.

The Grandmothers teach about the four phases of life, each contained within.

- Beginning, gestation: in the womb everything is equal. All is accessible to us. There is blossoming, purity, integrity.
- Separation and new growth.

- Empowerment. Holding on to the Vision.
- Fulfilment or Birth; self-realisation, listening to the shells to get back to the Essence and source – thus benefiting all sentient beings.

The cowrie, symbol of the feminine power of birth, rebirth, the womb or cocoon asks that we listen carefully to our authentic nature. 'Lohe-Lohe*' is to live in awareness and harmony with 'Mana**', the divine power infused in the natural world, of which our breath is a symbol. In Hawaii they were used against the poison of the centipede. They are good for sprains.

* Hawaiian, means 'Listen, listen' or 'Slowly, slowly'.
** Hawaiian, means 'Vital force'.

Using cowrie shells is like being cradled by the Goddess, creating a cocooning resonance.

Augers and Cones

Spiralling energy helps create change, releasing old patterns that no longer serve us and forming new ones that benefit us.

Cones help us in relaxation of the neck and shoulder area if applied using a gentle spiral motion.

The long narrow spirals of augers resemble the energy of the single pointed quartz crystal in which the atomic structure of the crystal moves in a spiral to the apex.

They bring a higher frequency of intent as the energy spirals in the body towards the centre of pain.

Ask your inner guides to bring you to the causal level, perhaps showing you a symbol that needs clearing.

Movement and life are synonymous, so that anything which prevents and obstructs it, by imposing rest and immobility, is the death principle – for what no longer changes, turns into decay. Conversely, that which is kept moving, circulating, is the life principle.

Symbolic systems such as the spiral in shells exist to help, develop, maintain and recover an organic way of life.

When we are willing to allow deep emotions to flow there is invariably a gift of love on the other side. Sorrow brings the tidings of joy. Becoming one with our feelings is a crucial step on the path of life.

With faith and hope a new revelation will gently come to heal our heart and soul. Let us imagine that the sea has claimed our tears and that the sun is drying our eyes.

All spiralling shells aid us in finding spiritual and emotional equilibrium within the realm of feelings. A profound change awaits us when we integrate a personal sense of empowerment with a serene understanding of the universal flow of life. Inner harmony can lead to divine bliss.

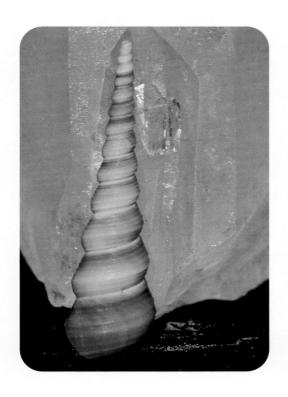

The Chambered Nautilus

N.B. As the nautilus is becoming rare, please read the chapter 'Information on Threatened Species.'

The chambered nautilus is one of the most beautiful shells, with deep sacred teachings. Its sealed internal chambers are formed in a perfect spiral, each being larger, with mathematical precision, than the preceding one. Its message to us is to let go of trivia and concentrate on the centre. The nautilus connects us to our own authenticity and to the oneness of all life.

The shell itself is large and coiled, off-white in colour, with distinctive tan flame-like radial bands. This outer coating is of a more masculine, powerful energy. Yet when this outer layer is removed we are graced by the beauty of its translucency, which very often captures rainbows of light. This nacreous inner coating teaches us to let go of the protective walls we have built around us and show our true self, our vulnerability, our hidden beauty, our softness. Love manifest in this spirit will bring change and growth.

We can be strong in our tenderness. Tenderness and power are meant to live together.

Safely, softly it tells us to remove the protective coating and show our tender feminine side.

From the still point, through the different chambers, we go out into the world and then return home to our divine essence.

'The chambered nautilus spirals around in perfect harmony enclosed in a shroud of banded white protection holding the luminescent Goddess surrounding the One example of ying Balance.'

Each chamber can represent a quality of life that we need and wish to live. I remember doing an exercise with the nautilus, holding it on my heart and feeling that I was navigating in the vulva of the sea. As I went through each chamber I opened to a deeper understanding of the feminine goddess energy – a transformation into receptivity, softness, vulnerability, trust, sensuality, and ecstasy.

The key message of the chambered nautilus is to trust in the reflection of total harmony and centering.

At One with the Breath of the Universe
The Ebb and Flow of the Ocean
Where Intake and Release meet.
I am Home – right and left in union.

The Conch

In ancient cultures by the sea and especially in island societies the conch, after the apex is removed, is used as a trumpet to announce the beginning of the day: The Opening of the Heavens.

Depending on where they are found, some conches spiral to the left and some to the right.

It was a beautiful and sacred experience for me as I was initiated into learning how to blow a conch. We had gathered as a small group on the sandy beach, a remembrance of Lemuria perhaps, or a sacred simple life. And there, after much practising, finally I was able to blow deep sounds to the sky, to the universe.

There I returned when my beloved teacher Lin passed on, wishing her good travels to the other shore through the breath and sound of the conch.

At the beginning of any healing ritual the conch is blown over the aura of the body to clear it, much as a Native American would use a feather, sweeping the sound, using the vibration, amplifying the energy vortex.

Before any meditation-healing it is good to focus on how we wish to use this journey. The power of intent, together with an attitude of gratitude for the experience to come, enhances and deepens our perceptions.

As we work with the seashells we remember that they come from the depths; just like lotus flowers, they are tools of transformation and sacredness.

We allow ourselves to be open to the spiritual water of universal love and divine healing.

One single shell

A simple way is to pick one shell, from several in a basket, and do a meditation with it.

Look at it carefully, observe and feel the colour, the design, the form, and then lie down with it. Put it on your body wherever it feels right at the moment, just as you would do with a quartz crystal or coloured stone.

Surrender and allow feelings, images, sensations to arise. Connect with Mother Sea, entering into communion and listening gently. Remember: Lohe-Lohe.

Opening and healing of the heart

Put four radiant shells such as scallops in a cross pattern over the heart centre. Add one spiral shell, such as small nautilus or cowrie or other shell in the middle. Also add radiant shells on each shoulder joints.

Breathe deeply, allowing emotions to surface and be released.

Sometimes during these sessions on the heart, guides of wisdom and love will appear such as dolphins, whales, and mermaids. Dolphins leap in the joy of the moment; they represent the intelligence of the universe. They remind us to play and let go of serious baggage, of too much thinking, to reconnect with our inner child. Whales speak of the wisdom of change, from the deep unconscious into the sunlight of higher revelations. Mermaids bring their nurturing love and remind us of the deep treasures buried within our own hearts.

Imagine the possibility of unlimited love, joy and wisdom. Let this powerful transformation lead you to emotional rebirth.

Believe in miracles.

Abdominal discomfort

This is a very effective pattern to use in cramps and abdominal discomfort tension.

Create a circle of five to seven radiant shells such as scallops or cockles surrounding a large cowrie. Place these on the area of discomfort while you lie down.

Breathe in light and release the pain or tension.

The number five, as found in the starfish, reveals the potential of creative mind. The number five is connected with freedom and unexpected changes on the path of life. The five-pointed star teaches birth, initiation, service, rest and transformation; evolutionary humanity; speaks of the union of earth and heaven. (The number seven, such as the seven-pointed star, symbolises the light of spiritual protection and guidance.)

This pattern restores harmony where there is tension.

As Nature is harmony and we as human beings are part of Nature, then innately there must be harmony. Healing is a return to harmony.

Headaches

A useful pattern for tension headaches is an alternate placement of scallops and small spiral shells around the head. The spirals can be any small shells, such as augers or mitres, but feel free to use whatever you have or whatever calls you.

If you are doing the pattern yourself, make a semicircle of the shells and then lie down with your head inside it. It's quite lovely to look at as it resembles a crown.

Breathe deeply... Breathe in light... Breathe out the tension... Remember that the recurrent moments of crisis are growth junctures which mark a release from one state of being and a growth or birth into the next.

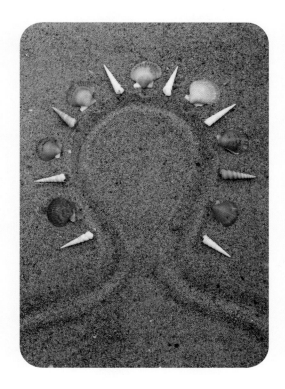

Relaxation

For general relaxation or meditation you can use as many shells as you wish. A pattern pleasing to the eye will also be pleasing to the body.

Create a circle or oval of shells to sit in or lie in. It is good to have at least one large shell for the crown such as a nautilus or conch, and a coral at the feet.

When tired or stressed add specific shells to the main areas of tension.

Use your creativity and let the shells guide you. Experiment to see how they feel to you. Be confident that there is no wrong way. Be sure to ask for their help and give them a blessing or thank them for their assistance.

Energising

If you wish for a more energising pattern, then add to the oval pattern of shells some cowries on either side, and place spiral shells on head, hands, and feet.

Imagine the energy circling in clockwise movements.

Breathe in the energy of the spiral.

Full healing body layout

It is very useful to do a full body shell layout to create specific energy changes in the body in various patterns. This can enhance the healing process and improve the energy flow. It also allows us to connect with the feminine or goddess essence of the shells.

The purpose of a healing ritual is to make us a more conscious agent of cosmic forces. It initiates the organism into an expanded and intensified participation in the workings of the universe.

As we attune ourselves to the various energies of Nature, we come into a 'resonance' of these elements and are brought into an at-one-ness, a return to harmony.

Thus with the aid of the shells and the sea we can heal and regenerate ourselves. The main idea is to create a relaxing, peaceful field of energy with the shells. The radiant shells are for flow and releasing tensions, the spiral shells for increasing intensity and for making a change in a pattern that has created pain or 'dis-ease'.

Here is an example of a full body layout. Most often I let my intuition guide me for each situation.

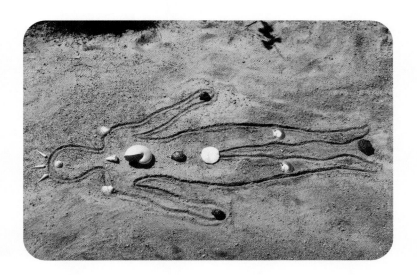

3 or 5 augers or spiral shells

1 mushroom coral

2 cockles or scallops

2 cone shells

1 nautilus or mushroom coral

1 cowrie

1 mushroom coral

2 cowries (in the hands)

2 cockles or scallops

1 red coral

(from left to right)

In this example I start at the feet and move up:

- A red coral between feet (you might use agatised coral instead)
- Two cockles or scallops on knees

- A mushroom coral on sexual organs for first chakra (you might use a brown cowrie instead)
- A cowrie on solar plexus
- A nautilus or mushroom coral on the heart centre (you might use a large spiral shell instead)
- A cone shell on the throat with another under the neck helps relieve tension (use one on each side of neck if that is uncomfortable)
- Two cockles or scallops on shoulders to enhance energy flow. Also can be added to hips
- A small mushroom coral or any other small spiral on third eye (you might use a white cowrie instead)
- Above the head: a crown of three to five augers or small spiral shells
- Hold a shell such as a cowrie in each hand. Any other shells can be added along the legs and arms
- Breathe deeply and allow yourself to be wholly receptive to the mysterious rhythm and magic dance of the deep waters.

This is only an example; please let your intuition guide you with the full body layout. The corals and nautilus I have used here are now classified as threatened species and should be bought only with extreme caution having checked the source. Please read the chapter on threatened species.

A trip to the beach:
a visualisation exercise

Create a circle of seashells to enhance the experience. Breathe
deeply three times. With each breath let your body relax and release
any tension you feel. Picture yourself joyfully taking your little child
self to the beach to play. Feel yourself expanding with each breath
you take.

See yourself on a beautiful sandy beach – one you have visited or
seen in a picture. Listen to the sounds of the waves gently moving
along the shore. Feel the sun warming your face and a breeze softly
blowing from the ocean, caressing you as you walk along the shore.
Feel the sand under your feet as it squishes up between your toes.
Notice your spreading footprints left behind you as you walk.

Now find a special spot where you can sit and look out to the vast
space of the deep blue water. Watch the waves breaking away from
the shore in their constant rhythm of ebb and flow. See them wash
away your footprints with their endless movement. Be aware how
relaxed and calm you have become with each movement of the
waves.

Watch the shoreline as a big wave hits the beach with a loud slap-
ping sound. As the water recedes you see a shell that has been left
on the sand, shining and wet. You receive it as a gift from Mother
Sea and move quickly to pick it up. It feels solid yet soft as you hold
it. Look at it carefully, its shape and pattern and colour. Hold it gently to your body as if it is hugging you. Listen with all your senses,
allowing your energy to connect with it. Feel the nurturing and sup-
portive essence of the shell. Acknowledge the gratitude you have for
it and express it to the shell. It seems to be giving you a message.

Allow yourself to ask for and receive any information the shell wishes to share with you and how you might use it. Experience your child self with the shell – the wonder of it.

Take as much time as you need before you return the shell to Mother Ocean. Gently bring your attention back to your body, move your hands and feet, and bring yourself back to the present.

Thank yourself for giving yourself a moment of rejuvenation and joy, and write down the experience to help ground and retain it.

Playing with a circle of friends and a shell

This is another fun way to use the shells with friends, seated in a circle. One special shell is picked from a basket to represent the hidden magic of life, and will be used as a means to access our inner selves. Everyone is told that the shell is magical and holds within it an undiscovered aspect of themselves that is ready to emerge!

Begin with a statement or invocation declaring:

'We in the circle acknowledge and accept the parts of ourselves that this shell can reveal, and we give thanks for the new insights given and received.'

As the shell is passed from person to person they are to say the first word that comes to them, without analysing or judging. Whatever image or phrase or symbol comes out is allowed.

The words or images or associations are significant to the people they come to, as they release energy and open new possibilities for each person who participates.

Have fun – give your imagination free rein.

It is with great joy in my heart that I offer you and share with you the wondrous healing, nurturing and transforming qualities of my Shell Essences.

These were created in the awesome 'Mana' power and beauty of Kauai, on the new Moon in Pisces, February 20, 2004 at sunrise – auspicious new beginnings.

Each Essence has a unique quality and gift, and comes with an appropriate affirmation to be said with intent as a prayer, whenever you take it. The Essences are a vehicle for the energy of the seashells, and can be used to intensify the work with the particular energies of special shells. They embody, emanate and transmit Mana, the energy or essence of the Sun as it rose in full majesty over the dark, mysterious, pearly waters of the night – the sky ablaze in a magnificent light-show of golden and pink rays blessing the new day as well as the luminescent rays of the New Moon shining and growing, the breeze though the palms, the sweet scent of plumeria flowers, the song of the waves on the shore, the Mana in the breath and the perfection, delicacy and exquisiteness of form and colour in the shells.

How to use:
A few drops of water under your tongue
A few drops on your hands
A few drops on your head.

Existing Essences, with appropriate affirmations, are:

Red Coral: 'I move and dance with life in joy; I bless my body with love.'

Sunrise Shell: 'I am enthusiastic about life, and filled with energy and love.'

Dark Tahitian Pearl: 'I call on the wisdom of the Divine Feminine within myself; I am open to receiving the gifts of the Great Mother.'

Cardium Cardissa: 'I love myself and I have the compassion and courage to fly.'

Jewelled Rainbow Abalone: 'I know my centre and extend myself in Full Rainbow to the Divine Mother, in total trust that I am loved and cared for by Her.'

Translucent Actor Top: 'I am at one with myself, focused and centred on the light, as I concentrate on my goal.'

Pecten Nobilis Red: 'I honour my body as the home of my spirit. I care for my body and am ready to release what no longer serves my wellbeing.'

Pecten Nobilis Yellow: 'I centre myself and trust my mind to be clear, peaceful, focused and knowing, like the sun.'

Pecten Nobilis Lavender: 'I aspire to the highest truth and open my heart to unconditional love.'

Trinity of the Three Colours: 'I am at one with myself, focused and centred on the light, as I concentrate on my goal.'

Essences to come: Mushroom Coral, Nautilus

You can order all these essences directly from Daya. Contact her by mail at her address in Hawaii for further information:

Daya Sarai Chocron · PO Box 1896 · Kapaa Hi 96746 · USA

The Legacy of the Sea

The Grandmothers taught that for women the best time to go into the sea for rejuvenation of their femininity was just before dawn, as the sky is still dark and as the first light arrives.

During one of my spiritual healing journeys with the shells I was told that it was time for me to move into a quiet space where I could receive. For so many years I had led groups, taught, been very active; and now was a time to live and re-experience my feminine receptive side.

Shortly after Lin finished teaching her series of classes, the house that I was renting by the sea was sold! So I found a lovely, smaller house by the river – ten minutes from the sea where it merged.

I began the daily ritual of driving to the sea, in the darkness, with a thermos of tea, my journal, a flashlight. It was an absolute awakening to be on the shore while the star Venus was still shining in the sky and enter the virgin water as the first light would come upon the earth. The sea felt like silk, pure and fresh from the night – a womb – a Mother with open arms unconditionally receiving, nurturing, and loving.

This became a blissful time for me. After my daily bath, I appreciated the warm tea. I would write in my journal and go on a walk along the shore looking for shells. I felt so loved and cared for by the Universe, nurtured; a true healing happened. A softness entered my heart and spirit.

Our legacy of the sea is harmony and balance, nurturing, understanding, wisdom and gentleness.

All nurturing comes from the ability to pay attention to our needs and feelings. If we are willing to nurture ourselves through connection to our Mothers Earth and Sea, we will know how to nurture others. This love we receive is the basis of beauty.

Thus, no matter what happens in the world, our heart has the capacity to remain open, serene, unafraid, and loving.

'The truth of love is the truth of the universe.
It is the lamp of the soul that reveals the secret of darkness.'
Kabir

Appendix to identify the described seashells

There are many different kinds of seashells, and the field of conchology is broad and complex. The aim of this book is not to be a professional seashell guide, but rather an easy-to-handle tool.

Below each of the two main seashell forms, radiant and spiral, we have listed as relevant all the shells mentioned in this book, with descriptions and photos of some non-endangered shells belonging to that family in order to aid you in collecting or buying them. One or two species have no picture; this is because these are rare or threatened species.

If you wish to research further, it will be helpful for you to know the family classifications as used in marine biology, so we have included these. Beneath the photographs we mention both the common name and the scientific name of each shell to aid in their identification.

If you are simply buying the shells you won't need their scientific names. If you find shells on the beach, the photographs will help you to identify them. However, for healing purposes you don't even need to identify them; it is enough to recognise the spiral form and the radiant form, so that you know which kind of energy emanates from them.

GOOD SEASHELL RECOGNITION GUIDES:

Shells, Graham D. Saunders, Usborne Spotter's Guides,
ISBN 0-7460-4576-X
Shells, S. Peter Dance, Smithsonian Handbooks,
Dorling Kindersley, ISBN 0-7894-8987-2

Radiant Energy Shells

CLAM

Habitat: Shallow water (fresh and salt). Clams can be found through-out the world.

Description: Clams are mostly oval shaped (with the exception of the razor clam with its elongated form). The term "Clam" is often used to refer to any bivalve that is not an oyster, mussel, or a scallop. Some clams produce pearls.

Scientific:
Class: Bivalve
Family: Can be found in different taxonomic families

Rose Petal Tellin, Purple Clam, *Tellina Lineata*

COCKLE

Habitat: Sandy bottoms, buried in the sand or mud, shallow water; world-wide.

Description: Cockles are heart-shaped (Cardiidae means 'heart'); the external shells are symmetrical and feature strongly-pronounced ribs. Cockles typically burrow using the foot, and feed by siphoning water in and out, sifting plankton from it. There are about 200 species in existence.

Scientific:
Class: Bivalve
Family: Cardiidae

Yellow Pricky Cockle, *Trachycardium muricatum*

LIMPET

Habitat: Rocky coast of most oceans of the world, dwelling attached to the rock.

Description: Limpets have cone-shaped shells and belong to the snail family. There are about 35 known species world-wide. When the limpet emerges into the air at low tide it creates suction with its shell to keep it attached to the rock and to prevent it from drying out. When the tide returns the limpet lifts its shell and continues to graze. They tend to return to the same place on the rock, sometimes even causing a visible 'scar'.

Scientific:
Class: Gastropod
Families: Patelliadae, Acmaeidae

Common Limpet, *Patella (Patella) vulgata*

MUSHROOM CORAL

Habitat: Indian and Pacific Oceans; can be found on soft seabeds in shallow and sometimes muddy reef water.

Description: True to its the name, the mushroom coral is oval in appearance with radiating skeletal walls (septa). This coral is attached to stony substrates only when it is young; growing, it becomes mobile and moves around on the seabed (as much as 30 cm a day). Mushroom corals don't live in colonies, but are solitary.

Conservation: Mushroom corals are listed in the Convention on International Trade in Endangered Species (CITES). This means trading in coral is regulated, and it is not permissible to take it back home as a holiday souvenir.

Scientific:
Phylum: Cnidaria
Family: Fungia

MUSSEL

Habitat: Lakes, rivers, creeks, tidal zones, oceans of the world, saltwater and freshwater. Attached to rocks and stones, or living in soft sediment like mud or sand in shallow water.

Description: Mussels have two close-fitting pear-shaped shells. Their colour may vary from purple or blue to brown, green or black according to their environment. Saltwater mussels belong to the taxonomic family Mytilidae, and freshwater mussels to the Unionidae family.

Scientific:
Class: Bivalve
Families: Mytilidae, Unionidae

Blue Mussel, *Mytilus Edulis*

RED CORAL

Habitat: Mediterranean, Cape Verde Islands and some parts of the Atlantic. Occurring in depths ranging from 10 to 280 metres, they prefer a dark environment, with a solid rocky seabed.

Description: Red corals are branch-shaped creatures. They form so-called coral reefs, building them from the skeleton of calcium carbonate they secrete. Living together in colonies, they provide a natural habitat for many other species. Their colour can vary from dark red to pink or white. They grow very slowly (1–8 mm a year) and live for about 75 years.

Conservation: The red coral is under threat from climate change as well as human action like pollution and over-exploitation. In some countries import and export of coral is restricted and needs authorisation.

Scientific:
Phylum: Cnidaria
Family: Gorgonacea
Name: Corallium Rubrum

SCALLOP

Habitat: Tropical and Polar waters. They can be found in shallow waters as well as in great depths and prefer tidal zones which protect them from strong currents.

Description: Scallops have a central adductor muscle and thus the shell has a characteristic central scar, marking its point of attachment. The shape of the shell tends to be highly regular, and may fit our standard image of a seashell. Scallops, unusually, swim by using their valves, rapidly opening and closing them and so moving backwards.

Scientific: *Class*: Bivalve. *Family*: Pectinidae

Pilgrim's Scallop, *Pecten Jacobaeus*

Austral Scallop, *Chlamys australis*

TUSK SHELL

Habitat: World-wide, living in the seabed sediment.

Description: Tusk shells have a curved tubular form open at both ends, resembling an elephant's tusk (hence the name). They are mostly small but can reach 15 cm long. They feed on microscopic detritus, sifting through the sediment with their tentacles.

Scientific:
Class: Scaphopoda
Family: All species of this class are called tusks

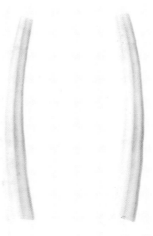

Tusk Shell

SUNRISE SHELL

Habitat: Typical Hawaiian shell which can only be found on Kauai.

Description: The sunrise shell is also called Langford's Pecten, and so belongs to the scallops. It is very precious and small in size (no bigger than a coin). It is called the sunrise shell because of its brilliant appearance, reminding us of the special energy of this time of day.

Scientific:
Class: Bivalves
Family: Pectinidae

Spiral Energy Shells

ABALONE
(Ear-shell, Paua-shell)

Habitat: Can be found all over the world, clinging solidly to rocks in sublittoral zones.

Description: Abalones have a mother-of-pearl interior and are rounded to an oval (resembling the shape of an ear). The body whorl has a series of holes near the anterior margin. The exterior colour varies from species to species.

Scientific:
Class: Gastropods
Family: Haliotis

Rainbow Abalone, *Haliotis (Paua) Iris*

AUGER

(Tower shell, screw shell)

Habitat: Dwelling in the sand or mud on the seabed and found throughout the world.

Description: As indicated by their name, augers resemble screws and have an elongated shape. They come in different colours and, depending on the family, they are either carnivores, catching their prey with stunning poison (Terebridae), or they feed on particles of detritus fallen to the seabed (Turritella).

Scientific:
Class: Gastropod
Families: Terebridae, Turitella

Screw Turitella,
Terebra Turritella

Marlinspike,
Terebra Maculata

Conch

Habitat: Indio-Pacific Ocean and Caribbean region. Sandy and algae-rich zones.

Description: The appearance of conches can vary, according to the exact kind. Common to all kinds is the mouth, which shows a flattened lip sometimes bigger than the shell itself. They have long eye stalks, a long and narrow aperture, and a siphonal canal with an indentation near the anterior end called a stromboid notch. Unlike most snails, which glide slowly across the substrate on their foot, strombids have a characteristic leaping motion, using their pointed, sickle-shaped, horny operculum to propel themselves forward in a leaping motion (Parker 1922). There are about 65 living species.

Scientific:
Class: Gastropod
Family: Strombidae

Purple Mouthed Stromb, *Strombus Sinuatu*

CONE

Habitat: Tropical shallow waters in coral reefs.

Description: As indicated by their name these snails are cone-shaped. The 400 to 500 known species show an extremely wide range of colours, patterns and sizes. Common to all cone snails are the characteristic tooth-like fangs they use as harpoons to catch and paralyse their prey. Depending on the species their venom can be strong enough to kill a human being in a short time. In the medical sector the venom of some cones is being studied, and it seems there might be some use for it as a replacement for morphine, or as part of a compound of remedies against Alzheimers, Parkinsons or epilepsy.

Scientific:
Class: Gastropod
Family: Conidae

Marble Cone,
Conus Marmoreus

Tessellated Cone,
Conus Tessulatus

COWRIE

Habitat: Commonly in the tropical regions, especially Maldives or East Indies, but also in temperate zones; very few species in cool water (European Cowrie) often under rocks.

Description: The shell is more-or-less egg shaped with a long slit-like opening. Their usually smooth, porcelain-like, glossy exterior is pleasing to the eye and shows a wide range of colours and patterns throughout the 250 known species.

Scientific:
Class: Gastropod
Family: Cypraeidae

Jester Cowrie,
Cypraea Scurra

Cribaria Cowrie,
Cypraea Cribraria

MITRE

Habitat: All over the world. Temperate and tropical waters under rocks, burrowed in the sand in coral reefs.

Description: Their elongated form is reminiscent of the shape of a mitre (peaked hat or head-dress worn by clergy such as bishops), hence the name. These shells show a wide range of colours and patterns. They are carnivores and feed by using their long retractable mouth.

Scientific:
Class: Gastropods
Families: Mitridae, Costellariidae.

Cardinal Mitre, *Mitra Cardinalis*

MUREX

Habitat: Tropical zones, Indo-Pacific, living in the tidal zone, among rocks or corals.

Description: The elongated shells are richly decorated with spines. Both inner and outer surfaces are often highly coloured. These carnivorous marine gastropods account for about 700 known species. The mucus of some species is the origin of the dye Tyrian purple (royal or imperial purple); very rare and expensive in former times.

Scientific:
Class: Gastropods
Family: Muricidae

Endive Murex, *Murex Endivia*

NAUTILUS

Habitat: Western Pacific, waters around coral reefs.

Description: The nautilus is similar in general form to other cephalopods, with a prominent head and undifferentiated tentacles. Nautiluses have up to ninety tentacles, although without suckers. The shell is calcareous and internally divided into chambers. Nautiluses swim by jet action using a fold in the mantle called a hypodome, and by pistoning water by head movements into and out of the living chamber. They are predators and feed mainly on shrimp and other small sea-life.

Conservation: The nautilus is not yet protected by CITES and is therefore widely collected by humans. In some countries export has been banned. This species is worthy of protection as it is one of the oldest species on earth, first appearing 550 million years ago during the early Paleozoic era.

Scientific:
Class: Cephalopod
Family: Nautilidae
Species: Pompilius

SCREWSHELL
See Augers

TRITON

Habitat: Warm and tropical seas all over the world, living in sandy bottoms.

Description: These shells are smoothly spiralling, and can be found in various colours and shapes, sometimes provided with strange little knobs or protrusions. These nocturnal carnivores catch their prey by immobilising it with their saliva.

Scientific:
Class: Gastropods
Family: Cymatiidae

Perry's Triton, *Cymatium Perryi*

WHELK

Habitat: Temperate and cold waters all over the world, living in shallow water but also in depths of up to 1200 m. They can be found in mud and gravel grounds.

Description: Whelks can be found in many different colours and shapes, and are large or small depending on their environment. Tropical whelks are brightly coloured and smaller than the Polar species. Both may be ornamented with tubercles along the shoulder. With around 800 species this family is extensive. Whelks are scavengers and carnivores, equipped with an extensible proboscis that is tipped with a file-like radula. The radula is used to bore holes through the shells of clams, crabs and lobsters. They also have a large muscular foot with which they hold their victims.

Scientific: *Class*: Gastropods. *Family*: Buccinidae

Winding Stair Shell, *Pugilina cochlidium*

Biological definitions of the two main classes of seashells

Gastropod

Most members have a shell, which is in one piece and typically coiled or spiraled, usually with the opening to the right. Several species have an operculum that operates as a trapdoor to close the shell. This is usually made of horny material, but in some molluscs it is calcareous.

Bivalve

Creatures of the Bivalvia class are known as bivalves because they typically have two-part shells, with both parts being more or less symmetrical. Bivalves are exclusively aquatic; they include both marine and freshwater forms.

Sources and interesting information sites

The descriptions in this appendix are in part taken from Wikipedia, the free encyclopedia. The following descriptions (in the body text): clam, cockle, limpet, scallop, abalone, conch, nautilus, whelk, gastropod and bivalve are licensed under the GNU free documentation licence and can be used as explained under:

http://en.wikipedia.org/wiki/Wikipedia:Text_of_the_GNU_Free_Doc umentation_License

http://en.wikipedia.org, the free encyclopaedia

www.gastropods.com, a very good site about gastropods with many pictures

www.marlin.ac.uk, a very informative site about seashells in the UK

www.marinebio.org, an interesting site about all sea-life

http://seashellworld.com, for both information and trading

http://waquarium.mic.hawaii.edu/, a site especially interesting for Hawaiian sea-life

http://www.geocities.com/slongrigg/index.html, a very informative site about seashells in the UK

http://nighthawk.tricity.wsu.edu/museum/ArcherdShellCollection/, very informative site about the Gladys Archerd Shell collection on the site of the natural history museum of Washington State University.

http://www.arkive.org/coral/Coral/coral.html, all about corals; very informative.

www.conchologistsofamerica.org, site with various information

Information on threatened species

In this book we mention different kinds of seashells and corals, many of which can be bought in shops or found on the beach. Nevertheless we would like to remind our readers about their responsibility to the environment and natural resources. Thus when beachcombing for shells, make sure these no longer host a living creature. When buying seashells in a shop, you might check that they were collected without the use of dredging machines or other destructive methods.

The main focus of this book is to disseminate the ancient wisdom of healing with seashells as taught by the Hawaiian 'Grandmothers'. This wisdom belongs to a time when humans were still living in harmony with the planet. Although we can't ignore the changes modern times have brought to our environment, we can choose to live in a more harmonious way. We all need to be aware of the responsibility we have in relation to our mother, our planet. We all need to be aware of our impact. Education is the key, and so in this spirit we are pleased to bring you additional wisdom about the environmental changes happening at the moment, and suggestions as to what you can do as an individual.

Some shells are listed under CITES (Convention on International Trade in Endangered Species).

Corals: Coral reefs are similar to our rainforests: they give a shelter to millions of different sea creatures, thus representing one of the most diverse habitats on this planet. Coral reefs are under threat from human action like large scale collection, dredging and pollution. The main cause for the contemporary dying off of coral reefs (through bleaching) is the global warming of the oceans. Corals are very sensitive to temperature changes.

The **red**, or **pink coral** mentioned in this book is not yet listed under threatened species, but should nonetheless be handled with care, because for some countries trade is restricted or import forbidden. Some other species of the coral family (fire coral or black coral) are listed under the CITES convention, and import is forbidden for 148 countries, including the UK, USA and Australia. The status of protection can change; for current information you might ask about special local restrictions in your area.

You might use alternative items like:
- The gemstone called 'agatised coral'
- The red coral essence produced by Daya (see chapter about essences).

Mushroom Coral is listed in the Convention on International Trade in Endangered Species (CITES) therefore international trade is regulated. This has happened as a result of so many tourists taking these corals back home as a holiday souvenir; but this practice is no longer sustainable.

You might use alternative items such as:
- The gemstone called 'agatised coral'
- The mushroom coral essence produced by Daya (see chapter about essences).

The **Chambered Nautilus** is mostly threatened through commercial fishing. In many countries export has been banned, but people still want to buy these shells because of their beauty. Unfortunately they haven't been protected by CITES yet, but we strongly recommend buying only those which are guaranteed not to have been live caught.

You might use alternative items like:
- Any big spiral shell
- The chambered nautilus essence produced by Daya (see chapter about essences).

If you're lucky enough as to already possess these shells, or live near a beach where you can still find them, of course you can use them.

For actual restrictions, especially concerning the import of seashells, check: www.cites.org

For the IUCN 'red list' of threatened species, check: www.redlist.org

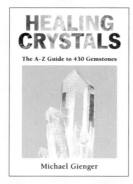

Michael Gienger
Healing Crystals
The A - Z Guide to 430 Gemstones

All the important information about 430 healing gemstones in a neat pocket-book!
Michael Gienger, known for his popular introductory work *Crystal Power, Crystal Healing*, here presents a comprehensive directory of all the gemstones currently in use.

In a clear, concise and precise style, with pictures accompanying the text, the author describes the characteristics and healing functions of each crystal.

Author's contact:
Daya Sarai Chocron · PO Box 1896 · Kapaa Hi 96746 · USA

For further information and book catalogue contact:
Findhorn Press, 305a The Park, Forres IV36 3TE, Scotland.
Earthdancer Books is an Imprint of Findhorn Press.

tel +44 (0)1309-690 582   fax +44 (0)1309-690 036
info@findhornpress.com
www.earthdancer.co.uk   www.findhornpress.com

EARTHDANCER

A FINDHORN PRESS IMPRINT